THE GAR
LITTLE BOOK OF
VERSE

Brian Lawless

ARTHUR H. STOCKWELL LTD
Torrs Park, Ilfracombe, Devon, EX34 8BA
Established 1898
www.ahstockwell.co.uk

Fifty per cent of the net profit from this book will be donated to
the Alzheimer's Society (Registered Charity Number 296645).1

ISBN 978-0-7223-5096-6
Printed in Great Britain by
Arthur H. Stockwell Ltd
Torrs Park   Ilfracombe
Devon EX34 8BA

CONTENTS

Preface   5

Chapter 1 – Spring
    The Spring   7
    The Slug   8
    Roses   10
    The Tip   11

Chapter 2 – Summer
    Beans   12
    Tomatoes   13
    The Bamboo   14
    The Lawn   16
    Hydrangeas   16
    The Rain   17
    Weeds   18

Chapter 3 – Autumn and Winter
    Bulbs   20
    Leaves   22
    The Freeze   24
    The Winter   26
    The Tree   27

Chapter 4 – Out of Season
    Herbs   28
    The Secateurs   29
    Hedges   30
    The Railings   31
    The Clean-Up   32

PREFACE

If you have picked up this book it almost certainly means that you also have a garden, window box or even a few pots dotted around – anywhere plant life thrives, survives or, at worst, dies!

Gardening, in all its forms, is very much a representation of life. There are highs, lows, ups and downs, successes and failures, frustrations and satisfactions. There is work (digging, planting, pruning, etc.), there is waiting for things to happen, and there is joy at eventually seeing lovely flowers and fruit arrive by virtue of your own efforts. There's a host of other delights too, such as sitting outside in the tranquillity of a warm summer evening and enjoying the garden view in the fading light with a beer or a wine – or even, as in my case, a cup of tea!

There is the love of seeing a beautiful rose, and the pleasure of cutting a single flower and presenting it to your loved one – a gift which can say so much. In case you are now seeing me as a sentimental old person, I'll balance that by saying there's also the hate of things, such as weeds which just won't submit to your destructive efforts together with slugs and snails and bugs which seem to be doing their level best to sabotage your efforts at every turn!

Perhaps a few, if not all, of the subjects raised in these little poems are familiar to you, having suffered or enjoyed similar experiences already!

This little book does not purport to be a literary masterpiece. I'm no Shakespeare, or even Ayres! However, I hope you enjoy it and that it raises a smile or two along the way.

Happy reading!

CHAPTER 1

SPRING

THE SPRING

The spring is great; it's time to plant.
Don't go too early – you just can't,
Because the frost might come and then
You will have to start again.

There's polyanthus, stocks and dahlia,
There's marigolds and big begonia,
There's geraniums and busy lizzie –
The choice will put you in a tizzy.

I've put some in – they look so fine,
They'll do me proud, they'll be divine.
I'll feed and water, then they'll grow –
My garden it will be just so.

A week's gone by – I'm going to see
Just what those plants have done for me.
Oh no! It's such a sorry tale:
The lot's been eaten by a snail.

THE SLUG

The slug is not a pretty thing –
It never makes us poets sing.
It slithers all around the place
And hasn't even got the grace
To leave my lettuces alone;
It bites them right down to the bone.

I suppose I should be much more kind,
Although I'm driven from my mind.
I plant and plant with so much care,
That slug will make me lose my hair (what's left of it!).
I'm going to the shed cos, well, it's
Time to break out those slug pellets.

ROSES

I think roses are so nice –
They really are my only vice.
They keep on blooming on and on;
It's only winter that they're gone.

I prune them back till they look sad –
It makes me feel so very bad,
But when the spring comes round, you see,
They start to bud, I'm filled with glee

Because I know that in a while
They're really going to make me smile.
When they bring forth their magic blooms
I'll jump for joy and lose my glooms.

THE TIP

Spring in 2020 was as weird as it could be,
For gardeners especially; read on and you will see.
The sun was out for weeks and weeks; the garden it did glow
With lots of flowers, fruit and veg, which need the sun to grow.

This all sounds good (indeed it was) – all were most impressed,
But all that glisters is not gold: there's problems there, you've guessed.
With all the foliage and stuff which needs a good old chop,
The garden waste began to grow – it really wouldn't stop.

But horror! All the council tips were closed. It had to be
With covid on the warpath, even gardeners must agree.
It would be foolish– nay, insane – to visit such a place,
To risk infection even with a mask upon your face.

Most gardeners keep compost bags to hide their waste away –
You'd have to have a huge amount to keep that lot at bay.
The problem is to find a space to keep those bags around.
The pile grew big, and bigger still – at least that's what I found.

But then at last the councils opened up their tips to us;
We loaded cars up to the hilt and went without much fuss,
Until we got there just to find a queue for miles and miles.
Every driver ground their teeth and lost their eager smiles.

But all things come to those who wait, and, thirty minutes on,
In you went to grab a space and soon the lot was gone.
The car was empty, you felt great, and off you went at last –
A weight was off your shoulders and the crisis it had passed,
Until the next time!

CHAPTER 2

SUMMER

BEANS

Come on, beans – do your stuff.
This really isn't good enough!
My neighbour Bill's beans are quite tall,
But you, my friends, are far too small.

I feed and water every day,
But still you won't come out to play.
I guess I'll have to wait and frown,
But still I think you'll let me down.

Last year I had some bumper crops
And boasted that my beans were tops;
Now all I do is sit and cry –
I know I must eat humble pie.

Whatever pie I eat will be
Unaccompanied, you will see.
My diet will be pretty lean.
What is in it? Not one bean!

TOMATOES

I've got loads of plants this year –
I've always held tomatoes dear.
I've moved them round to get the sun;
I've nurtured each and every one.

I talk to them both day and night
To make sure that they turn out right,
Full of taste and big and red –
I'm proud of my tomato bed.

It's time to pick the lovely things –
My family will eat like kings.
But what is this? This can't be right –
The blooming things have got the blight!

THE BAMBOO

I like bamboo –
I hope you do too.
It makes a swish sound
As it blows around.

It's tall and it's green
And I can't be seen
When I'm feeling quite rude
As I lie in the nude.

I'm sunbathing, you see!

THE LAWN

The sun is up, the lawn is brown –
This weather really gets you down.
If only it would rain and then
It might turn back to green again!

HYDRANGEAS

I love hydrangeas – I think they are great.
I've got one that's early; I've got one that's late.
It means I have blooms for seven months each year –
I boast to my neighbours, of that there's no fear.

I know that they don't like me much, of that I am quite sure –
When I ring on their bell, you see, they don't answer their door.
I think I can remedy this very awful rift:
I'll buy them all hydrangeas. That should give them quite a lift!

THE RAIN

It's good for the garden's what they say
Just as the sky begins to grey.
They won't say that in three weeks' time –
They'll be moaning, "It's a crime!"

It won't slow down – there's floods galore.
It's forecast to rain more and more.
"My garden is in bits," they say.
"I wish this rain would go away."

I'm waterlogged, my blooms a wreck –
And Him above, I'll break His neck!
If He won't stop and give us sun
I think I'll go and get my gun.

And then we'll see who's in charge here,
But first I'll stop and have a beer.
To calm me down, to help me think,
It always helps to have a drink.

But what is this? The sky looks clear –
That calls for yet another beer.
The sun's come out, it's warm at last,
My worries are all in the past.

WEEDS

I hate weeds with all my might –
The blooming things, they're just not right.
I spray and spray near every day –
Those darned things just won't go away!

I've tried with bark, but that's no use;
I've even shouted mild abuse.
I pull them out, then count to ten –
The blank things just grow back again.

I've covered them with plastic sheeting,
But the pause is only fleeting
Till they force their way right through –
I just don't know what else to do.

I think I've had enough of that;
I'll just give in, and buy a flat.

CHAPTER 3

AUTUMN AND WINTER

BULBS

I've got spring bulbs in my shed – they're hanging in a stocking.
My partner took her leg out first or else it would be shocking.
They're hanging there to dry, you see, till I plant them again,
And I don't have to buy some more with money down the drain.

I replant them every year – I'm waiting for the autumn.
They come up with their blooms for me – it's years since I first bought 'em.
Those daffodils – delightful things – I view them at my leisure,
And tulips with their petals bright they give me lots of pleasure.

The hyacinths are gorgeous and I love them every one
As they reach out and try to get the warmth of the spring sun.
But the best of all, I have to say, what keeps us both on track:
My partner and her leg, you see, they get their stocking back.

LEAVES

I think I'll have a bonfire. I'll get out my old brazier;
But then again, perhaps I won't. I've never felt more lazier.
My garden's full of leaves, you see – it's autumn and they've dropped.
I've watched them from my bedroom window; now it seems they've
stopped.

I've got to shift them somehow, that's why I thought of fire.
If I could be bothered I could make up such a pyre.
The irony I have to face, it seems so sad to me:
The blooming things all gathered there, they're not from my own tree.

They've come in from the bloke's next door – that's why it's so unfair.
I get quite mad when I look out and see them lying there.
I think I know just what I'll do (it seems to make most sense):
I'll pick them up and chuck them back, right across his fence.

THE FREEZE

I don't do much to the garden in winter – it's cold.
The reason for that, to be frank, is I'm old.
I've slaved through the autumn, the summer, the spring,
But winter's the time when I don't do a thing.

The worst thing in winter is always the freeze –
It nips at the nose and it bites at the knees.
It's time to sit down by the fire for heat
And roast up some chestnuts – that just can't be beat.

I'll take it quite easy this time of my life.
I think I'll watch telly and talk to the wife.
I think that the garden and planting will keep –
I'm going upstairs to have a long sleep.

THE WINTER

It's wintertime, it's snowed, you see, and all the ground is white.
I'm going out for a walk – it all looks very bright.
My woolly hat and scarf are both in place, so I am warm;
I hope I have a long, long walk before another storm.

As I walk on I look around at all the bleakness there –
I'm waiting for a warmer time when things are not so bare.
But then I get a nice surprise – it makes me gasp and stop.
I'm filled with joy, my heart is full, I see the first snowdrop.

THE TREE

My tree is a palm –
It does me no harm
Apart from the leaves,
Which drop in great sheaves.

It's getting too tall.
When the postman does call
He says, "Lookie here, mate –
That palm tree ain't great.

"If that was to fall
I could do bugger all!
If it lands on me
I'd be buggered, you see." (He swears a lot!)
I said, "Push off, you clown –
It ain't coming down."

I called a surveyor –
An opinion purveyor.
He came just last week –
He looked quite a geek.
But he said, "It's OK,
So be on your way."

That told 'im!

CHAPTER 4

OUT OF SEASON

THE HERBS

I once grew herbs – I have to say, it made me feel quite **Sage**.
This use of double meaning words helps me feel half my age (I wish!).
I suppose that writing this will somehow help me **Parsley Thyme**
–
You readers may well think that I'm committing verbal crime.

My girlfriend, lovely **Rosemar**y, is looking at TV –
She's watching **Corri And 'Er** mind's on that, not me.
So I'm seeing my mate **Basil** and we're going down the **Bay**
To have a swim although it might be **Chilli** so they say.

I have a son called **Dill** Boy (I'm sorry, *Only Fools*).
He thinks he's at that **Love Age** now and makes up his own rules.
He always needs a **Chick or 'E** is desperate, so it seems.
Valerian Saffron are his favourites in his dreams.

He went off to America – it was to the North West.
He went to stay in **Oregan, oh** at a girl's request.
She left him when he got there – he felt so put upon.
The last thing he was heard to say was "Where's my **Tara Gone**?"

Lots of poets writing verse, they make a proper **Mint**,
But though I've penned this little book I bet I end up skint.

I think I'll stop there!

THE SECATEURS

Secateur is a French word, so I am told.
I learnt that in school before I grew old.
It means just 'to cut', which explains quite a lot.
There's quite a neat handle on the ones that I've got.

My son bought them for me a few years ago –
It was for my birthday; they cost lots of dough.
I'm very pleased with them although they are green,
So when I look for them they just can't be seen

As most of the things in the garden are *vert* (more French!)
And I guess at my great age I'm not so alert.
But writing this down I've had a good thought:
I'll tie a red ribbon around them, quite taut.

That means I can find them wherever they've gone,
Even if I've not got my glasses on.
I'm really quite clever – there's no flies on me.
I think I deserve a nice cup of tea.

Decaf, of course!

HEDGES

My garden has some hedges – they seem to grow so fast.
I'd like to get them taken down, but there, the die is cast.
I used to trim the things myself – it was a massive job.
When I used my big trimmer, it made my brain cells throb.

It's one of those extended ones – it reaches to the sky.
It's good for what it's meant to do – it trims the bits up high.
It's powered by electricity, but not a cordless one.
The lead gets tangled up a lot – it really is no fun.

Not only that, it's heavy: it seems to weigh a ton.
The whole thing is a battle – one I've never won.
I've thought about just what I'll do to make sure I do win.
I think I've got the answer now: I'll get a youngster in.

THE RAILINGS

There are railings round my garden – they do look rather smart,
Especially when I've painted them. It is a work of art.
The trouble is the paint only lasts a couple of years
Before it starts to peel away – it leaves me all in tears.

I have to rub it down each time before I paint again;
But every time I want to start, it seems to want to rain.
It happened to me yesterday – I was mired in grief and sorrow.
I know what I'll do today: I'll leave it till tomorrow.

THE CLEAN-UP

My patio gets filthy – my standards are quite low:
I only get to clean it, well, each two years or so.
I've tried with all the chemical stuff that's in the garden shops,
But I've found that they are no use, and then my spirit drops.

The only thing that does the job is a power washer,
So I went round and borrowed one from my good friend old Nosher.
I stuck the hose upon the thing, the other end on the tap,
Then I plugged the electric in and fell into the trap

Of thinking it was easy, but it was far from that.
The water shot out really fast and nearly drowned the cat.
It bounced against the garden wall, rebounded back on me –
I was so wet I thought I had been swimming in the sea.

I rushed indoors like a drowned rat and reached out for a towel;
I dried myself, got changed and then went back out feeling foul.
I'd put on my old cagoule with hood around my head;
My bottom half had waterproofs that I kept in the shed.

And in the end I tamed the thing and got the job all done.
I have to say, it looked quite good although it wasn't fun.
In two years' time, when I want it to be clean as a new pin
I'm giving up and what I'll do is get an expert in.